I0419836

Quote Octopus
Melbourne, Victoria, 3053
Australia
www.quoteoctopus.com

Discipline is the bridge between goals and accomplishment.

Jim Rohn

To be yourself in a world that is constantly trying to make you something else is the greatest accomplishment.

Ralph Waldo Emerson

You have to remember that the hard days are what make you stronger. The bad days make you realize what a good day is. If you never had any bad days, you would never have that sense of accomplishment!

Aly Raisman

The greatest accomplishment is not in never falling, but in rising again after you fall.

Vince Lombardi

Being busy does not always mean real work. The object of all work is production or accomplishment and to either of these ends there must be forethought, system, planning, intelligence, and honest purpose, as well as perspiration. Seeming to do is not doing.

Thomas A. Edison

It had long since come to my attention that people of accomplishment rarely sat back and let things happen to them. They went out and happened to things.

Leonardo da Vinci

The supreme accomplishment is to blur the line between work and play.

Arnold J. Toynbee

A great accomplishment shouldn't be the end of the road, just the starting point for the next leap forward.

Harvey Mackay

Nothing builds self-esteem and self-confidence like accomplishment.

Thomas Carlyle

The entrepreneurial life is one of challenge, work, dedication, perseverance, exhilaration, agony, accomplishment, failure, sacrifice, control, powerlessness... but ultimately, extraordinary satisfaction.

David S. Rose

I seriously feel like the best days are ahead, and I like the idea of getting to do everything I did before but with more knowledge, experience, and street smarts. There's a certain love, appreciation, and gratitude that you have at 40 that you don't have when you're younger, and it makes every accomplishment feel so much better.

Jennifer Lopez

Nothing stops the man who desires to achieve. Every obstacle is simply a course to develop his achievement muscle. It's a strengthening of his powers of accomplishment.

Thomas Carlyle

I saw as a teacher how, if you take that spark of learning that those children have, and you ignite it, you can take a child from any background to a lifetime of creativity and accomplishment.

Paul Wellstone

Well-being cannot exist just in your own head. Well-being is a combination of feeling good as well as actually having meaning, good relationships and accomplishment.

Martin Seligman

Telling lies is a fault in a boy, an art in a lover, an accomplishment in a bachelor, and second-nature in a married man.

Helen Rowland

I would like to be remembered as a guy who had a set of priorities, and was willing to live by those priorities. In terms of accomplishments, my biggest accomplishment is that I kept the country safe amidst a real danger.

George W. Bush

I started reading about people of great accomplishment... and it dawned on me suddenly that the person who has the most to do with what happens in your life is you.

Benjamin Carson

You get whatever accomplishment you are willing to declare.

Georgia O'Keeffe

There is a real magic in enthusiasm. It spells the difference between mediocrity and accomplishment.

Norman Vincent Peale

Children love and want to be loved and they very much prefer the joy of accomplishment to the triumph of hateful failure. Do not mistake a child for his symptom.

Erik Erikson

Nothing splendid was ever created in cold blood. Heat is required to forge anything. Every great accomplishment is the story of a flaming heart.

Arnold H. Glasow

I have always been more interested in experiment, than in accomplishment.

Orson Welles

Every great work, every big accomplishment, has been brought into manifestation through holding to the vision, and often just before the big achievement, comes apparent failure and discouragement.

Florence Scovel Shinn

The feeling of accomplishment welled up inside of me, three Olympic gold medals. I knew that was something nobody could ever take away from me, ever.

Wilma Rudolph

All the breaks you need in life wait within your imagination, Imagination is the workshop of your mind, capable of turning mind energy into accomplishment and wealth.

Napoleon Hill

Accomplishment is socially judged by ill defined criteria so that one has to rely on others to find out how one is doing.

Albert Bandura

All money means to me is a pride in accomplishment.

Ray Kroc

Your identity is firmly anchored in Christ's accomplishment, not yours; his strength, not yours; his performance, not yours; his victory, not yours.

Tullian Tchividjian

I grew up as a sports fan, and I know that a hall of fame is very different than an award for being the best of the year. It's a nod to the longevity of our accomplishment.

Chuck D

Self-image sets the boundaries of individual accomplishment.

Maxwell Maltz

Everybody starts at the top, and then has the problem of staying there. Lasting accomplishment, however, is still achieved through a long, slow climb and self-discipline.

Helen Hayes

Life is an accomplishment and each moment has a meaning and you must use it.

Jeanne Moreau

The great accomplishment of Jobs's life is how effectively he put his idiosyncrasies - his petulance, his narcissism, and his rudeness - in the service of perfection.

Malcolm Gladwell

Today, the biggest challenge we must meet is the one we present to ourselves. To not become a nation that places entitlement ahead of accomplishment. To not become a country that places comfortable lies ahead of difficult truths. To not become a people that thinks so little of ourselves that we demand no sacrifice from each other.

Chris Christie

I don't have any feeling of accomplishment about anything unless there's a lot of risk to it.

Mario Andretti

When your dreams include service to others - accomplishing something that contributes to others - it also accelerates the accomplishment of that goal. People want to be part of something that contributes and makes a difference.

Jack Canfield

Nothing stops the man who desires to achieve. Every obstacle is simply a course to develop his achievement muscle. It's a strengthening of his powers of accomplishment.

Eric Butterworth

If you can react the same way to winning and losing, that's a big accomplishment. That quality is important because it stays with you the rest of your life, and there's going to be a life after tennis that's a lot longer than your tennis life.

Chris Evert

Love in marriage should be the accomplishment of a beautiful dream, and not, as it too often is, the end.

Alphonse Karr

But with the right kind of coaching and determination you can accomplish anything and the biggest accomplishment that I feel I got from the film was overcoming that fear.

Reese Witherspoon

When Oscar Niemeyer died on December 5, 2012, ten days before his 105th birthday, he was universally regarded as the very last of the twentieth century's major architectural masters, an astonishing survivor whose most famous accomplishment, Brasilia, was the climactic episode of utopian High Modern urbanism.

Martin Filler

Winning the Royal Rumble is as big an accomplishment as anything.

John Cena

When you do a play, you have the kind of nightly feeling of accomplishment. But you also have the daily dread of the doing it every night. And because you're doing the whole thing every day, it's like climbing up the mountain every single night. With a movie it's like climbing the mountain very slowly, over months of filming.

Jesse Eisenberg

I've photographed just about everyone in the world. But what I hope to do is photograph people of accomplishment, not celebrity, and help define the difference once again.

Richard Avedon

Blessedness consists in the accomplishment of our desires, and in our having only regular desires.

Saint Augustine

Torment, for some men, is a need, an appetite, and an accomplishment.

Emile M. Cioran

I think that anything that you do, any accomplishment that you make, you have to work for. And I've worked very hard in the last ten years of my life, definitely, and I can tell you that hard work pays off. It's not just a cliche.

Cameron Diaz

For all the tribulations in our lives, for all the troubles that remain in the world, the decline of violence is an accomplishment that we can savor - and an impetus to cherish the forces of civilization and enlightenment that made it possible.

Steven Pinker

To be loved is important as is having a sense of accomplishment but to love is equally important in life especially when it is combined with taking action to do something for someone else to make their life better.

Richard Kiel

A good game gives us meaningful accomplishment - clear achievement that we don't necessarily get from real life. In a game, you've beaten level four, the boss monster is dead, you have a badge, and now you have a super laser sword. Real life isn't like that, right?

Jesse Schell

People now feel time accelerating. Lists allow them to feel some sense of accomplishment.

David Viscott

We are deeply conditioned against unconditionality because we've been told in a thousand different ways that accomplishment always precedes acceptance, that achievement always precedes approval.

Tullian Tchividjian

Spending is not caring. Spending is what politicians do instead of caring. Spending more does not guarantee success. Politicians like to measure spending because it is easier than measuring actual metrics of accomplishment.

Grover Norquist

Some people ask, 'How do you attract the young and so many different people when your poetry is complicated and different?' I say, 'My accomplishment is that my readers trust me and accept my suggestions for change.'

Mahmoud Darwish

My contribution I hope is to get people to eat full-flavored food. If I could come away with that alone, that would be a fantastic accomplishment. I'm also very proud of being a very American chef.

Bobby Flay

Only by strict specialization can the scientific worker become fully conscious, for once and perhaps never again in his lifetime, that he has achieved something that will endure. A really definitive and good accomplishment is today always a specialized act.

Max Weber

If I'd have went on the ice when this thing happened, someone would have speared me or something. It's a great feeling of accomplishment and pride. They had to do it; it was their moment.

Herb Brooks

An uplifting sense of purpose is more than an impetus for individual accomplishment, it is also a necessary insurance policy against expediency and impropriety.

Gary Hamel

My greatest sense of accomplishment has come from having two amazing sons, but it's also a paradox in that the times when I felt like the biggest failure have been times when I felt like, as a parent, I wasn't making the right decisions or succeeding in the way that I should.

Michael Franti

Who knows better than artists how much ugliness there is on the way to beauty, how many ghastly, mortifying missteps, how many days of granitic blockheadedness and dismaying ineptitude there is on the way to accomplishment, how partial all accomplishment is, how incomplete?

Tony Kushner

My most important professional accomplishment to date is the ability to keep working with absolutely no skills whatsoever.

Colin Mochrie

A miracle... my biggest accomplishment is my marriage so far. Because it's hard, everyone knows it's hard.

Gwen Stefani

Making it to the NFL is a huge accomplishment. Making it in the NFL is a huge accomplishment, but I haven't done that yet. No matter how many games we've played, it's still hard to figure out when you've made it in the NFL.

Robert Griffin III

Today, we are on a path of decay. We are seeing the book close on five decades of accomplishment as the leader in human space exploration.

Eugene Cernan

It is through accomplishment that man makes his contribution and contribution is life's greatest reward.

John Portman

Making the playoffs three consecutive seasons is a great accomplishment.

Pau Gasol

I feel a tremendous sense of accomplishment. Everything is in tune: the voice, the type of music, who I am and who people think I am.

Sarah Brightman

For the division of labor demands from the individual an ever more one-sided accomplishment, and the greatest advance in a one-sided pursuit only too frequently means dearth to the personality of the individual.

Georg Simmel

The mindset of chasing that next #1 record doesn't exist for me anymore. It's more about being a well-rounded entertainer than being a pop artist. Obviously, it would be wonderful to have a hit record but I don't base my happiness on that anymore. It's about the accomplishment of a project that satisfies me. I just want to enjoy the ride.

Donny Osmond

Everyone wants to be paid well - I know that I certainly do. But there are lots of other satisfactions that we get from our work. To feel needed. To feel accomplishment. To believe that our work matters. Being a lawyer gives you a rare chance to experience that kind of success.

Jeffrey Toobin

Having a better and more productive life than my monster father has been my most significant accomplishment.

Stephen Hunter

I think my playing has been orchestral throughout the years, and this is another way of expressing that. But I primarily see it as the ultimate accomplishment of a musician. Composing makes me feel like I've finally gotten all the way up the ladder as a musician.

Tony Williams

Accomplishment is such a patronizing, dangerous word, isn't it? I haven't really accomplished anything. The most accomplished thing I've done is to have lived this long - 81.

Patrick Macnee

I don't have muscle tone. I'm just flab. I'm not a daredevil. I don't like pain, I don't like cold, I don't want to feel exhausted. But the sense of accomplishment is something I've never felt before, in a physical sense.

Charlene Tilton

When we protect children from every possible source of danger, we also prevent them from having the kinds of experiences that develop their sense of self-reliance, their ability to assess and mitigate risk, and their sense of accomplishment.

Gever Tulley

Philosophic meditation is an accomplishment by which I attain Being and my own self, not impartial thinking which studies a subject with indifference.

Karl Jaspers

A remarkable thing about the Silicon Valley culture is that its status structure is so based on technical accomplishment and prowess.

Jaron Lanier

I look upon another's insistence on the merits of his or her life - duties, intellect, accomplishment - and see that most of it is nonsense.

Harold Brodkey

Egypt has been a partner of the United States over the last 30 years, has been instrumental in keeping the peace in the

Middle East between Egypt and Israel, which is a critical accomplishment that has meant so much to so many people.

Hillary Clinton

My children without a doubt are my greatest accomplishment. If I did nothing else I would feel just having and raising them would be enough. The rest is icing.

Andie MacDowell

I worked in sales. It was definable, it had a quantifiable approach to accomplishment that had a great deal of importance to me. It had a degree of clarity that I loved. And of course, it was core.

Anne M. Mulcahy

The greatest feeling of accomplishment for me is the fact that I was an athlete who was somewhat disabled.

Bill Toomey

Hey, I think it's easy for guys to hit .300 and stay in the big leagues. Hit .200 and try to stick around as long as I did; I think it's a much greater accomplishment. That's hard.

Bob Uecker

There's a strange sense of accomplishment in making an independent film. Everything's against you; there's no time, and even less money - you bring a bottle of glue, chip in twenty bucks, and hope you all make it through the day. If you manage to finish it and it actually turns out to be pretty good, it's thrilling.

Eric Stoltz

You can have meaning, accomplishment, engagement and good relationships, even if you are dull on the positive affect side.

Martin Seligman

Being varied is something I do instinctively and naturally. I feel a tremendous sense of accomplishment.

Sarah Brightman

Once a popular Alaska governor with a modest record of accomplishment, Palin could conceivably revive her reputation in this era of short memories. But it's hard to imagine her name atop the GOP ballot in 2016, when a cast of heavyweights who sat out 2012 will be vying for the nomination.

Ron Fournier

Health care reform, the marquee legislative accomplishment of the Obama administration's first term, was passed before we entered the world of divided government.

Eliot Spitzer

Being a mother is by far my greatest accomplishment.

Isla Fisher

Moreover, the accomplishment of Russia's aims has been greatly simplified by the fact that we have heretofore offered the world no practical antidote for the Russian poison.

James Forrestal

In Japan, mothers insist on achievement and accomplishment as a sign of love and respect. Thus to fail places children in a highly shamed situation.

Michael Lewis

My parents did a great job raising me and my two sisters. We all graduated from high school and we all graduated from college. So, to be a good representative of my family is probably my greatest accomplishment thus far.

Robert Griffin III

My first novel, 'The Lions of Lucerne,' just poured out of me. It was an amazing feeling of accomplishment. My biggest fear and therefore my biggest obstacle to becoming an author had been, 'What if I spend all that time and the book is no good?'

Brad Thor

Any form of a winning record in the conference is an accomplishment.

Jordan Knight

You would have to say his number one accomplishment has been to inspire a sense of confidence in the country. That confidence, that optimism, not only gives President Obama a political cushion, but it could have a real world economic impact.

George Stephanopoulos

Part of me believes that the completed record is the final measure of a pop musician's accomplishment, just as the completed film is the final measure of a film artist's accomplishments.

Jon Landau

My conviction of the necessity of further legislative provisions for the safe-keeping and disbursement of the public moneys and my opinion in regard to the measures best adapted to the accomplishment of those objects have been already submitted to you.

Martin Van Buren

There's something that feels more organic about watching a stunt that's done by you. There's also a feeling of accomplishment doing it yourself.

Cobie Smulders

My biggest accomplishment was playing 'Lark' on the daytime drama Port Charles because it was the most regular acting job I have had, and I had to step in and fill someone else's shoes.

Amy Weber

I can now successfully drive a stick. That's a huge accomplishment.

Shannon Miller

Wins are the most important measure for goalies, I think. Certainly it's a great accomplishment.

Curtis Joseph

The love of these people and of my fans mean more than any award or special accomplishment.

Wynonna Judd

I think I usually play the woman that, after the person tries to go for some extraordinary feat of romantic accomplishment, they happily wind up with me.

Jessica Hecht

I've never worked to make money. I understand we've got to eat and all that, but I never said I want to be a multimillionaire or a billionaire. To me, that's of no significance. I work to have the accomplishment.

Bob Parsons

My education in the public schools of New York City between 1932 and 1944 was an excellent preparation for a life in science. Because of the Depression, these schools were able to attract a remarkably talented and dedicated collection of teachers who encouraged their students to strive for the highest levels of accomplishment.

Robert Fogel

There is a price to pay for accomplishment.

Edwin Louis Cole

My biggest accomplishment has been making a transition from athlete to author.

Kareem Abdul-Jabbar

Although it was a great accomplishment to win a gold medal, as soon as they put it on you, that's it; your career is over.

Sugar Ray Leonard

Conquering America for a U.K. artist is incredible because that's what everybody wants and dreams about. The accomplishment is dominating a market which you aren't familiar with.

Rita Ora

I'm less worried about accomplishment - as younger people always can't help but be - and more concerned with spending my time well, spending time with my family, and reading, learning things.

Jonathan Safran Foer

Obama's victory in November 2008 was a historic political accomplishment.

John Podhoretz

Hitherto I have courted Truth with a kind of Romantick Passion, in spite of all Difficulties and Discouragements: for knowledge is thought so unnecessary an Accomplishment for a Woman, that few will give themselves the Trouble to assist us in the Attainment of it.

Mary Astell

Republicans always try to paint Democrats as weak on defense. This time, they can't. After all, Mitt Romney's idea of an overseas accomplishment is sending U.S. jobs there.

Chuck Schumer

Carole King's second album, 'Tapestry,' has fulfilled the promise of her first and confirmed the fact that she is one of the most creative figures in all of pop music. It is an album of surpassing personal-intimacy and musical accomplishment and a work infused with a sense of artistic purpose. It is also easy to listen to and easy to enjoy.

Jon Landau

Even on education, his one accomplishment, the Leave No Child Behind Act, and he has left it unfunded.

Sidney Blumenthal

But clearly the fact that we've gone from zero Iraqi security forces on duty in May to up to 200,000 today is an enormous accomplishment, but it's not enough.

John Abizaid

I'm a songwriter; that's where it starts. I love writing with someone that shares that same feeling of accomplishment. I'll play music for my fans as long as they'll listen, but I fancy myself as a writer first.

Randy Houser

There is something very intriguing about, for example, the sense of accomplishment that a small child has, which you might be able to reduce to aggression and libido, but which might also have some independent existence.

Peter Gay

A nobler example, because a less personal one, of the pinch of poverty, is when it prevents the accomplishment of some cherished scheme for the benefit of the human race.

James Payn

The biggest accomplishment, in racial terms, for Barack Obama was being elected. He had to overcome his blackness to be elected. He climbed the Mt. Everest of American politics, becoming an historic first.

Randall Kennedy

I find hunger more interesting than accomplishment.

Simon Van Booy

What middle-income Americans want most of all is a job. We need a generous safety net for the most vulnerable in our society, but for most people the biggest social accomplishment that we can help them achieve is a good-paying job.

Joseph M. Kyrillos

I didn't want people to think of me as someone who wasn't impressed with a silver medal, because obviously that's a huge accomplishment, and I was so happy. It was more about me just being not impressed with falling at the Olympics in my last event.

McKayla Maroney

I was a 'Big Brother' fan. I thought they were better musicians than their detractors claimed, but more to the point, technical accomplishment was not something I cared about.

Ellen Willis